The Kids'
Library of
Personal Safety™

A Kid's Guide
to Staying Safe at

PLAYGROUNDS

Maribeth Boelts

The Rosen Publishing Group's
PowerKids Press™
New York

Published in 1997 by The Rosen Publishing Group, Inc.
29 East 21st Street, New York, NY 10010

First Edition

Book Design: Erin McKenna

Photo Illustrations and Credits: Cover background and pp. 12, 16, 19, 20 by Seth Dinnerman; p. 4 by Ira Fox; p. 7 Jeffrey Myers/FPG International Corp.; p. 8 © Stephen Simpson/FPG International Corp.; p. 11 by Michael Brandt; p. 15 by Carrie Ann Grippo.

Boelts, Maribeth, 1964–
   A kid's guide to staying safe at playgrounds / by Maribeth Boelts.
      p.   cm. — (The kids' library of personal safety)
   Includes index.
   Summary: Offers tips on how to keep safe at a playground, including using the swings, seesaws, and other equipment safely and not talking to strangers.
   ISBN 0-8239-5081-6
   1. Playgrounds—equipment and supplies—safety measures—Juvenile literature. 2. Playgrounds—safety measures—Juvenile literature. [1. Playgrounds—Safety measures. 2. Safety.] I. Title. II. Series.
GV426.B64 1997
796'.06'8028—dc21

                                      96-30003
                                          CIP
                                           AC

Manufactured in the United States of America

Contents

Kevin and Jenna

Kevin unpacked the last box in his room. "I'm done with my room. How about you?" he asked his sister Jenna across the hall. They were moving into their new house.

"I'm ready to go too," she answered. "I just hope that this playground is as good as the one in our old neighborhood."

"I saw it yesterday. It looks even better than the old one," said Kevin.

Jenna went to find her dad. "Hey, Dad! Kevin and I think you need to take a break from all this hard work. Let's go to the park!"

◀ Discovering and learning about new places can be exciting.

Is My Playground Safe?

Playgrounds are fun places. But they need to be safe too. These **guidelines** (GYD-lynz) can help you tell if your playground is safe.

- What is on the ground underneath the playground **equipment** (ee-KWIP-ment)? Woodchips, sand, pebbles, or rubber are great. **Concrete** (KON-kreet) or packed dirt are very hard and can hurt you if you fall.
- Don't use equipment that is broken or rusty. A grown-up can tell you what's safe.
- Is the playground clean? Look out for garbage and broken glass.

Some playgrounds use materials such as ▶ woodchips to make the ground safer.

The Safe Way to Play

There are right ways and wrong ways to play. The right way means following the rules so you stay safe at the playground.

- Be sure that a grown-up is there to watch you.
- Tell your parent where you will be and when you will be back.
- Only visit the playground during the day.

With your parent, decide on the best **route** (ROWT) to the playground. Stick to that route. Avoid shortcuts, which can be **dangerous** (DAYN-jer-us).

◀ Always travel with friends when walking to and from school or the park.

Swings

Everyone likes to have fun on the swings. To stay safe, always sit down on the seat and hold onto the swing with both hands. Wait until the swing stops before you get off. When you are walking near the swings, leave lots of room between you and the person who is swinging. If a friend wants to swing next to you, that's great. Make sure she has her own seat, and don't hold onto each other's swing.

The safest way to swing is by ▶ holding on with both hands.

Slides

There are straight slides, bumpy slides, and slides that make you turn around in circles. Which kind do you like best?

On every slide, use the ladder to get up to the top. Don't climb up on the slide itself. When you get to the top, sit down and wait until the slide is clear before you go down. Always slide down feet first. At the bottom, move out of the way so the next person can have a turn.

◀ Always sit down when sliding down the slide.

Seesaws and Monkey Bars

If you want to play on a seesaw, you and your friend should each sit on one end and take turns pushing off gently from the ground with your feet. When you're finished, tell your friend that you're ready to get off. Then you can both make the seesaw even with the ground and stand up together.

Monkey bars are fun to play on with your friends. But it's important to be **aware** (uh-WAYR) of where other kids are playing or swinging. Make sure the bars are not wet or slippery from rain. You could slip and fall.

Learning new tricks on the monkey bars ▶
means learning how to be safe too.

Accidents Can Happen

Sometimes accidents happen and kids get hurt at the playground. If you see someone who is hurt, the first thing to do is stay **calm** (KALM). The hurt person will feel better if you are calm. Then call to a grown-up or go for help. If you are with another person, send that person for help while you stay with the hurt person. Don't try to move someone who is hurt. If he is bleeding, use a cloth or his own hand to press on the cut until help arrives.

◀ Try to stay calm if you hurt yourself at the playground.

Danger: Strangers

Strangers (STRAYN-jerz) are people you don't know. Some strangers look nice, but they could try to hurt you.

If a stranger comes to the playground, tell a grown-up right away. Stay away from the stranger and never take money, gifts, or rides from him or her. If he or she wants to talk to you, walk away fast. If you are scared, leave the playground. Go home and tell your parents.

It could be dangerous to talk to a person you don't know, even if he looks like a nice person. ▶

Protect Yourself

Here are ways you can **protect** (pro-TEKT) yourself at the playground:

- Always go to the playground with another person.
- Don't take candy, money, or rides from anyone unless your parent says it's okay.
- If a stranger tries to talk to you, walk away.
- Your body belongs to you. If someone tries to touch you in a way that makes you **uncomfortable** (un-KUMF-ter-bul), say "No!" in a loud voice. Then run away to a grown-up that you know and trust.

◀ Tell a grown-up if someone you don't know makes you feel nervous, scared, or uncomfortable.

A Great Choice

Playgrounds are great places to run, play, and pretend. At a playground you can make new friends and **exercise** (EK-ser-syz) your body. Playing at playgrounds is a great way to stay **healthy** (HEL-thee) and have fun.

If the weather is bad, there are indoor playgrounds that can be just as much fun. So why not turn off the TV, grab your mom or dad, and head for the playground?

Glossary

aware (uh-WAYR) Knowing what is going on around you.

calm (KALM) Peaceful and quiet.

concrete (KON-kreet) A very hard material made of cement, sand, water, and gravel.

dangerous (DAYN-jer-us) Something that can cause harm.

equipment (ee-KWIP-ment) The swings, slides, and climbing bars that make up a playground.

exercise (EK-ser-syz) The use of your body to make it stronger and healthier.

guideline (GYD-lyn) A rule or direction to follow.

healthy (HEL-thee) Good for your body and mind.

protect (pro-TEKT) To keep from harm.

route (ROWT) The path you take to get somewhere.

stranger (STRAYN-jer) Someone you don't know.

uncomfortable (un-KUMF-ter-bul) Feeling scared and unsure of yourself.

Index